God's Poems

WOMAN MAN SPIRIT

LOVE LAMONE

To order additional copies of this book, contact:
Xlibris
844-714-8691
www.Xlibris.com
Orders@Xlibris.com

ISBN: Softcover   978-1-6641-8552-4
        EBook   978-1-6641-8551-7

Print information available on the last page

Rev. date: 07/16/2021

Contents

AFFIRMATIONS

APHORISM

PRAYERS

POEMS OF LIFE

By:

---------Love Lamone---------

Is changing my life

I don't try to continue in strife
I can see more clearly now
I seek to know the way by the sweat of my brow
For I take care of myself and others I pray
So we can all rejoice and see another day

Is teaching me how to Love my wife

I will be with her for the rest of my life
Now I have a better marriage than ever before
We now live in harmony and have closed that awful door

Wisdom to understand my wife

And our longevity to live our lives
Her understanding me and my understanding her
And the peace that comes has made us wise
Therefore when we seek to love
We'll find eternal life

My children

The children I was with
And the children I left behind
I had to realize that they were all mine
I finally found them one by one
And show them all my love, daughters and sons

Sustaining me when my Life was a mess

All of my wrong doings I must confess
If it hadn't been for my perseverance to know the truth
I would have ended up screaming at the roof
I would not be a writer now; or a poet, singer, or musician,
A creative Artist, husband, father, or friend

Life is a mystery

When you don't know what is happening
What will you end up doing
Life is a mystery and a result of your choosing
Teaching me the mysteries of the way, the truth and the life
Is the only way that I can get it right

For teaching me

I must agree is the only thing that set me free
Not to be prejudice or treating people bad
Is the only way not to be sad
Life lessons are a rewarding thing
Take heed to them and then we can sing

To obey is the hardest to do

Following the Law of the Land...is my question for you
Obeying the stop signs, policemen and our elders to
We must encourage each other towards the ladder of success
Put your best foot forward and GOD will do the rest

For my enemies I pray

And "Bless" them daily, for that's the right way
When we look in the mirror what do we say
Are we looking at ourselves changing day to day
We can seek to answer many, many questions
But what is the result of our daily suggestions

For my favorite fruit –

Watermelon, grapes, pears and mango
Coconut, apples, and green melons in tow
I enjoy Gods fruitful vines
And am grateful for its blessings Devine
Fruit is energy and health to my body
So that I won't have to take a toddy

For my friends

I am so happy to have dear and loving friends
It is said show yourself friendly if you want to have friends
It is so easy to be mean and angry all day
I don't think that a friend would want to stay
We must also love our neighbor as our self
Listen we are people not an elf
Kindness is not just for Holidays
Be kind always and let's meet new friends

Well-being

I'm thankful to be in health
So I always think that way
We must remember to think positive
For it pays off one day
To think lovely is a key to long life
In changing your thoughts you'll have fewer vice

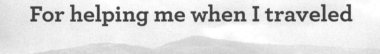

For helping me when I traveled

On the road we all want to be safe
So many of us are in the fast race
We never think about an accident twice
I'm talking about living and not about mice
When we look at our life we need consider it so
We also want to arrive safely at the end of life's road

I am thankful for LOVE

Love is spirit and not a dove
How many have walked hand in hand
Looking for this or that; maybe the latest brand
What is our life's assignment; do we know
Perhaps a search for realignment might cause an overflow
HOLD ON
How do we know where to go or what to do
When we find LOVE we'll no longer be a fooled

That day I lost my way to someone's house

Then I could not find the directions in my blouse
I know I would have gotten in trouble if I went there
I was lost for so long that I did not care
It was a bad house of people but how was I to know
I was given safety in the wind and snow

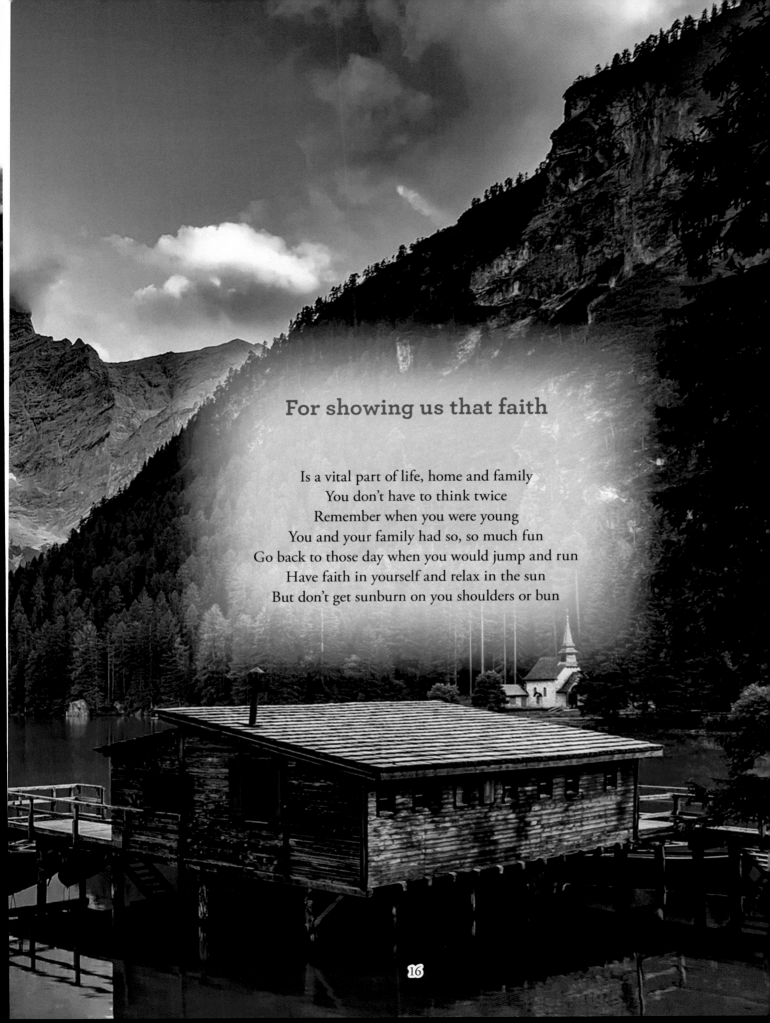

For showing us that faith

Is a vital part of life, home and family
You don't have to think twice
Remember when you were young
You and your family had so, so much fun
Go back to those day when you would jump and run
Have faith in yourself and relax in the sun
But don't get sunburn on you shoulders or bun

My mother always helped me

She pointed out my faults to help me grow
To see me through a life she loves me so
Through ups and downs and all the frowns
I know how much she loves me now I'm grown

For the truth that there are

Many people in the world
White People, red people, yellow people
Brown people and black people
Mankind was created colorful
And that is good!

For the ugly, the pretty

And the in between
We were all created the same
Imagine how dull life would be
If we all had to come down the chimney

For the help to not tell lies

And exaggerating the issue
So many even pick up the tissue
Tears in their eyes is not a surprise
They don't tell the truth
Even when they lose their tooth
Just be honest and stop telling lies
Then you will not have to dry your eyes

For Oats, grain, honey, wheat, corn, wine

Milk, the butter, eggs, sea salt, the herbs
Barley, flour, oil and the water
And for teaching me how to eat
To sustain and benefit my body I greet
Study what is for your body best
Meditate and let GOD do the rest

For the apples that I ate as a little boy

I always played outside and not with toys
I would play all day and those apples
Were the most delicious thing that I would have
I love apples to this day and they are
Healthy for you and me to eat

For protecting me from the brick

The fall, car, gangs and the bad women
Life has had many challenges
But when I fell out of the tree
And didn't even hurt my knee
And when the boy threw a brick and missed
And when I could not sleep
A mystery came over me
Life has many challenges

From my Dad, Joseph Louis Duskin

He took me fishing a lot
He taught me so our fish would not rot
I went with him almost everywhere
He also taught me not to have fear
To this day I love to fish
And my dad also taught me his favorite dish

For the married couple that gave me

The sockeye salmon sandwich whose house was on top of the hill
This is how all this happened
I could see their house from my third grade classroom window
My teacher was curious to see what I was looking at
I showed her the house on the hill. It was a long distance from the school
But I and my friends went all the way up the hill to that house during lunch
When we finally reached the top I saw the man and woman eating lunch
They saw me; I ducked down behind the wall that hid me
When I looked up, the man handed me a sandwich. It was so delicious.
I remember that taste to this day. I ran back through the woods,
Across the dangerous street back to school before the bell rang
I was so happy that people of another race could be so nice to me

For protecting me

From so many diseases
We often take for granted and many teases
That we will always be young don't ignore
The fountain of youth many have searched for
Words of wisdom for all even those of wealth
Is to take care of ourselves and our health
Stop smoking, drinking and living a wild life
Because when you are older you may pay twice

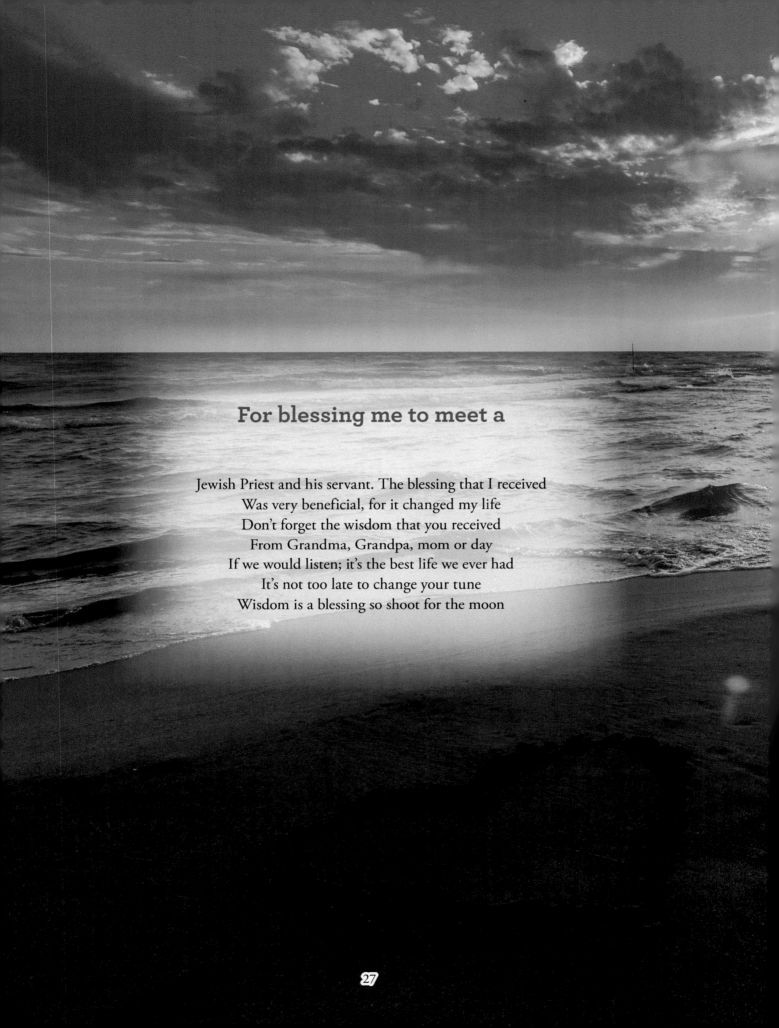

For blessing me to meet a

Jewish Priest and his servant. The blessing that I received
Was very beneficial, for it changed my life
Don't forget the wisdom that you received
From Grandma, Grandpa, mom or day
If we would listen; it's the best life we ever had
It's not too late to change your tune
Wisdom is a blessing so shoot for the moon

For my Dad, Joseph for he expounded on

The Word of God and showed me how a man should live
Take heed to those teaching and recall the past
Take hold of today for tomorrow will also pass
We will be rewarded for our life's work, be serious don't laugh
Don't be nervous or fearful we are people not calfs
Remember those lessons and we'll be successful to
Set your goals in life, you have been taught what to do

From my Mother, Bessie

For assisting my Dad in guiding us all to righteousness
Those inspired teaching were rich not spineless
I remember the many errors I made
My mother always said your bed is where you laid
She meant that your reward to according to your doing to
Don't slip because you will have it coming to you

For a good mind

A mind that remembers the Sabbath Day
And keeps it Holy
There are thing in life where you won't worry
Doing good always is the best thing to do
So that life consequences won't trouble you

For other races of mankind

What a beautiful rainbow
Since you are not God
It is not yours to decide or rob
We can all get along
If we choose to we can all be strong

For everlasting life

A Gift
Who would reject the best life
Only someone who doesn't know the truth
Ask GOD he will show you the way, the truth and the life

For Gods children

The assembly of the righteous
We are all one body, the righteous
There is no need to fight about who will succeed
If we work together no matter what the creed
All will be supplied to meet every need

For changing me

I was headed down the wrong roads
Life a frog or a toad
GOD changed my life from being mean
To a child of worship and I now sing

For healing me a thousand times

In ways I did not know about
You're the greatest Doctor
You made us and can save our lives

For teaching me how important a

Husband is in the earth. Like GOD who is a Husband/Father
I want to be just like GOD
(Those who want to learn how to be a husband
Should look at GOD, He is the greatest truth and example)

For showing me the woman who

I should not marry because she would not make a good wife
I am so grateful
Because I asked GOD he showed me my wife
And we are together happy and dedicated

AFFIRMATIONS

By:

-------Love Lamone-------

SIN, Inc...

Before Adam sinned
Someone is about to attack
Everyone is against everyone
Go and sin no more!
Am I innocent?
-HEALING EFFECT-
Who made you sin – the world, the darkness, or self?
-ALL THREE-
Tell death – to go to hell. Use your way of authority...
Sin and sickness go too
Are you trying to make me sin
-FEAR NOTHING BUT GOD-
Just heal the good and the bad
Heal everyone who wants healing
Oh! Remember to heal yourself to

What Do You Want

Did you come to me to teach me how to sin
How to get sick and ultimately die
What did you come to me to do?
Why did you come into my life
What do you want with me...

Why Are You In My Life

Tell me
Why are you in my life?
To do what
To hurt me
Did I ask you to come to me?
Did I call you or invite you?
Did I ask you to help
Or mess up my life —or?

The Mirror

I looked in the mirror and said
Who in the hell are you?
I have never seen you before...
-THE QUESTION IS-
Did you ask this because you are old or
Is it because you have lead a life of sin

God, Said Ask...

Did you mess up my life
Because you didn't have a life
Or were you angry at life
Because my life is intact
Are you a blessing or a curse
What are your intentions
Let me ask you this
Who are you anyway
Tell me the divine truth
If you don't tell me
I'm going to ask you to leave me right now
I don't know you
And you don't know yourself

Did God

Did GOD tell you to come to me
Well did HE
Are you in my life to cause
Confusion, havic or evil...

Question

I have a question to ask you
Why did you want to meet me
What is your divine reason
You must have a divine reason
If you don't know you reason
Then just tell the TRUTH

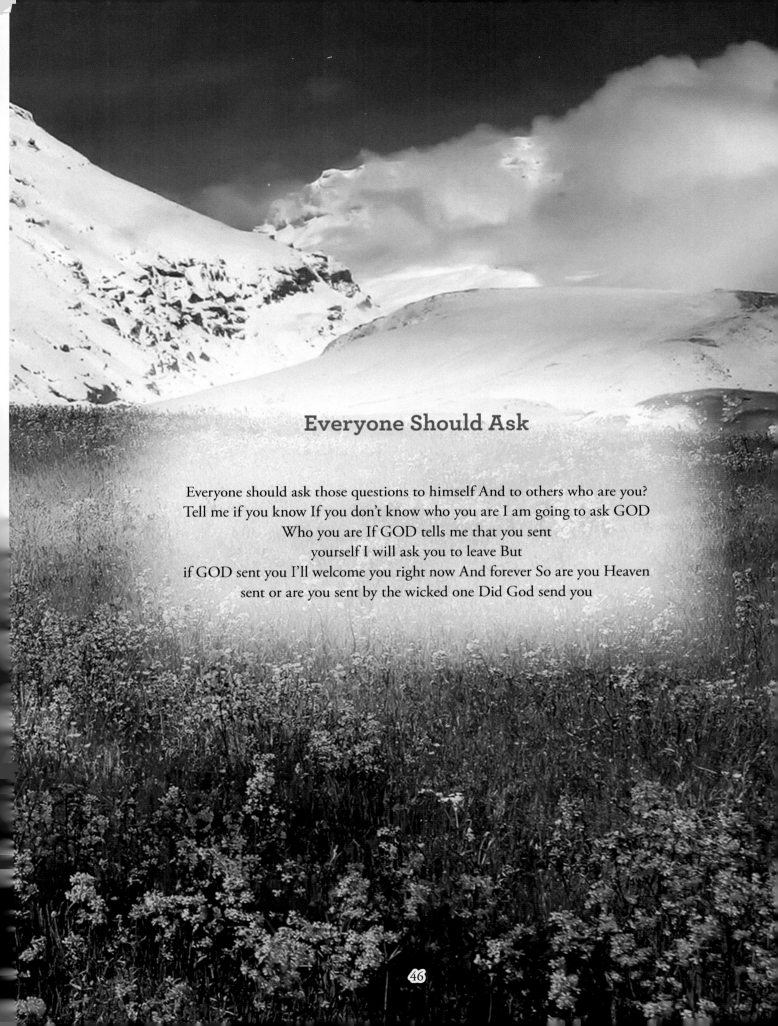

Everyone Should Ask

Everyone should ask those questions to himself And to others who are you?
Tell me if you know If you don't know who you are I am going to ask GOD
Who you are If GOD tells me that you sent
yourself I will ask you to leave But
if GOD sent you I'll welcome you right now And forever So are you Heaven
sent or are you sent by the wicked one Did God send you

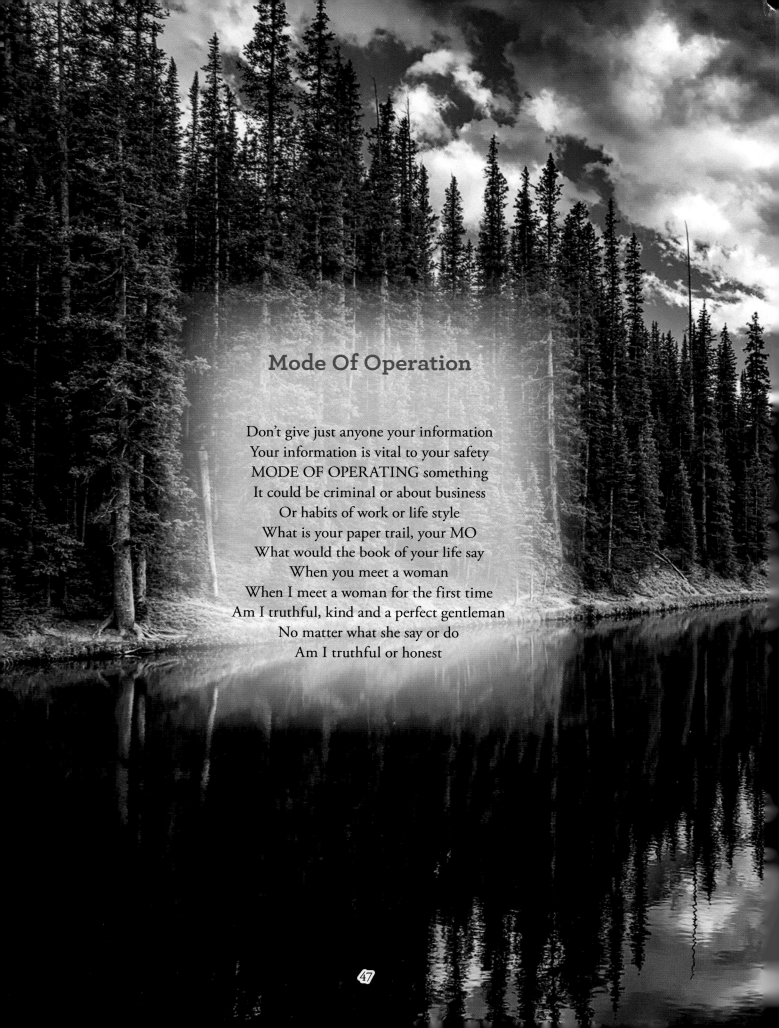

Mode Of Operation

Don't give just anyone your information
Your information is vital to your safety
MODE OF OPERATING something
It could be criminal or about business
Or habits of work or life style
What is your paper trail, your MO
What would the book of your life say
When you meet a woman
When I meet a woman for the first time
Am I truthful, kind and a perfect gentleman
No matter what she say or do
Am I truthful or honest

You Messed Up My Life

You messed up my life
For thirty years
So why did you do this to me...
Answer me...
-ANSWER-
It takes two to dance...
And by the way
I had help

Tell Me

Tell me everything
You can about yourself
Then I will look you up
And find out
What kind of life
You're been living, lying or dying

Did You Ask God

Lord, I'm really fond of this lady
Can you tell me more about her
She might not want to be with me
Or wan me to know her right now
GOD I'm looking for my soul mate
Is it her. I'll wait on your word

Are You Married

Hi, what's your name
You look beautiful
My name is Martha what's your name
My name is Daniel
Are you from this area
No I'm just driving through
Well are you married
Yes I am
Well GOD bless you and him

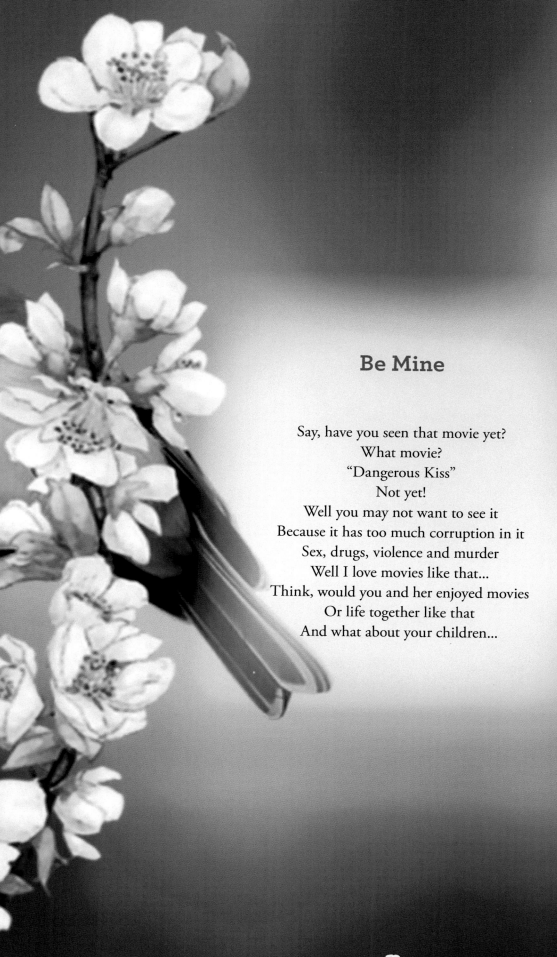

Be Mine

Say, have you seen that movie yet?
What movie?
"Dangerous Kiss"
Not yet!
Well you may not want to see it
Because it has too much corruption in it
Sex, drugs, violence and murder
Well I love movies like that...
Think, would you and her enjoyed movies
Or life together like that
And what about your children...

Cook For Me

Are you looking for a wife
To fulfill your life?
Are you seeking someone to
Cook, clean, wash clothes
Baby sit and dust...
If so, roll you sleeves up and help...

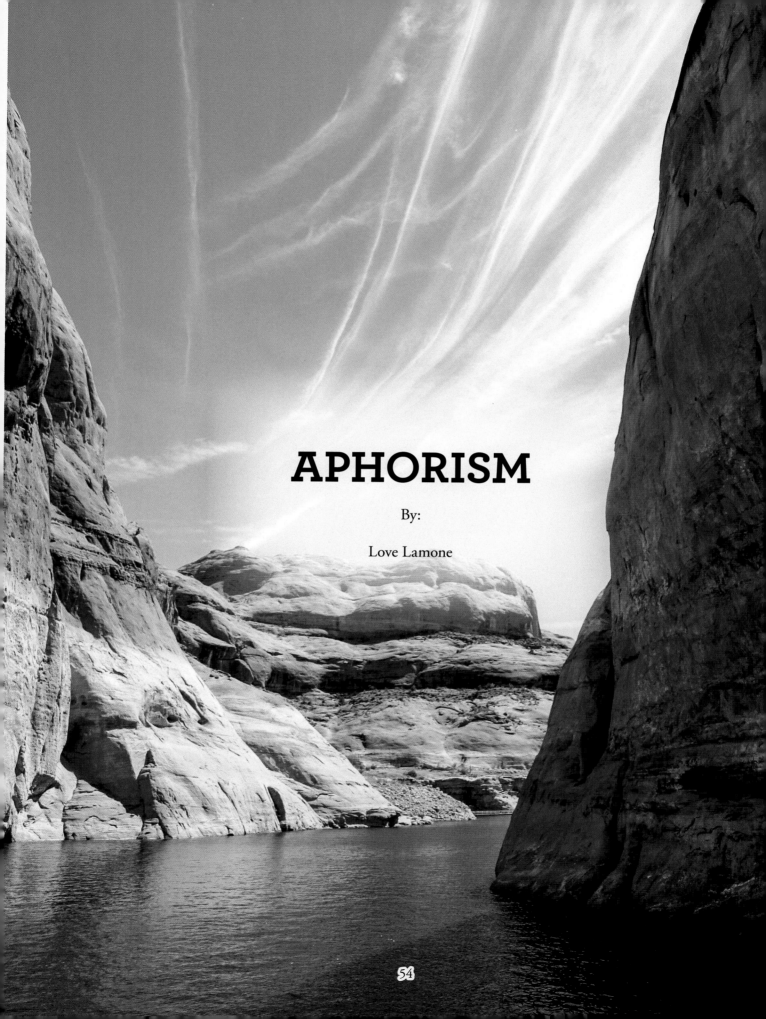

APHORISM

By:

Love Lamone

Dominion Over Flesh

What lead you astray. Are you a fool
Do you want to die and be destroyed for ever
What makes you fearful and depressed
Is it your own way of thinking
Do you go right to GOD
You're unwillingness to hear and be saved
Do you use your power GOD gave you
Or are you afraid to stand in the evil times today
Can you walk away from the evil of life
And run to GOD for safety and be healed

The Great Falling Away

I went to church, but no one was there...
I sat down and I waited
I looked around, I walked around
I was afraid-of what? What was I afraid of?
It was quiet in church...
Then I saw a dark tall preacher-he was crying
Save me, Save Me
I am blind and I can't see...save me
Everyone has run away...
I said, but Sir you are a preacher, you should save me...
He said I am a liar not a preacher
What made you think I was a preacher
Well...you are wearing a black suit

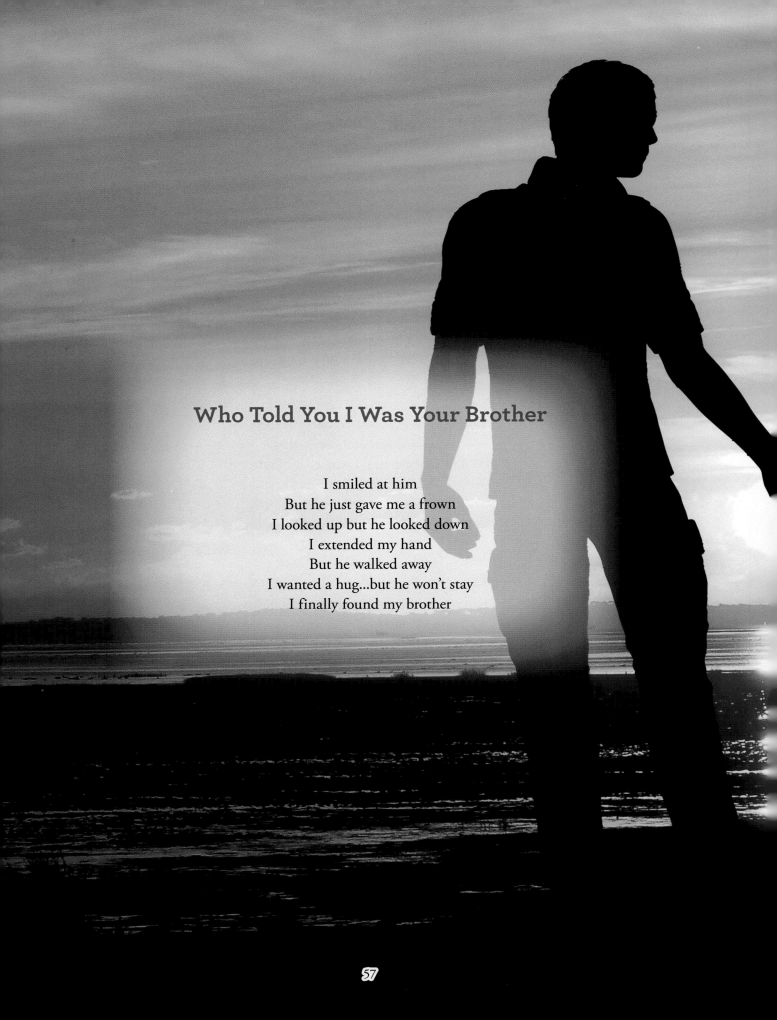

Who Told You I Was Your Brother

I smiled at him
But he just gave me a frown
I looked up but he looked down
I extended my hand
But he walked away
I wanted a hug...but he won't stay
I finally found my brother

Marry Me

Marry Me, Marry Me...
And You'll never be hurt again...

Yours for Life

I will be yours for life...
But don't ever let me be free
Keep me under lock and key...

I Promise

I promise, I promise!
But Wait...
I'm going to get a Bible
And a Judge and a Lawyer
And also your X-wife

One and Only

My One and Only Lover
I feel so brand new
So real inside...
I've never felt like this before
Until I met you...
Hello! Hello! Hello!
Are you there

LOVE

Love is for the warm
And healing, healing, healing...
When am I going to be healed?
When you start to love
You will be healed

A Walk

A walk in the park...
I'll be your best friend
I'll love until the very end
I'll walk in the park
While it is sun shinning...
But if it rains...

Remember Me

Remember me when I am old
Our talks, our walks
The dining, the fun
And the years gone by...

Just Think

Just think!
If I love everyone and GOD
I can live forever and never die!
I will be a Spirit of Love

Believe In Me

Believe in me...
And you'll never die
Lord, what do you mean?
I am Life Everlasting
I am Life!
If you love me...
You can not die...
You will be a part of me
You will fall asleep

Rich Man Poor Man

<u>The Poor Man</u>
I'll give you all I've got
What do you have she asked
Nothing but Love...

<u>The Rich Man</u>
I'll give you all I've got
What do you have she asked
Money...

Poor Man Rich Man

<u>The Poor Man</u>
Sweet heart, I'll find a job
And we'll have money, food, clothes
And we'll have shelter
And a beautiful life together
And Love forever

<u>The Rich Man</u>
I have money...
Take it or leave it

Man and Woman

GOD gave man
The most beautiful flower on earth...
But he forgot to water the flower
So it withered away...

A Kiss

May I have a kiss Mademoiselle?
Sir did you ask my father for my hand?
Do you want just one kiss?
Or kisses forever...

PRAYERS

By:

- - - - - - -Love Lamone- - - - - - -

Eternal Love

Eternal Love All Everlasting.
We lift up your name forever Father of Light,
Creator of heaven and earth.
Praise your Holiness GOD of gods,
healer of the darkness.
In the congregation I'll play music of delight.
Lord heal our unbelief and help
us understand the right way.
Lord heal the land and the people, Lord of Love.
Give us a well spring of life and aid us in troubles Father.
Save us today, tomorrow and forever and ever.
Thank you Lord of Light, teach us to live,
love and learn every single day.
Thank you Father

The End of Time

The end of what?
Better the end of a thing
Than the beginning thereof

Adam

Where was Adam

When the devil called Eve his wife...
Men listen, carefully
Don't leave your woman friend
Or your wife in the hand of the devil
So that it's bad & evil
If you do the demon will come to her...
Then there will be nothing you can do

Body Mind Soul and Spirit

Body mind soul and spirit
What more can we want
For heaven's sake!
With our bodies we enjoy all things
Just think - keep thinking
Don't stop, think...
Now our mind just look
At how we use our mind
Over and over again and again
It seems like we never stop
Even when we are sleep our minds
Are still dreaming, still working
But what about our soul and spirit...
When and how do we use
These two entities
We have every single day
What are we here for
Consider, our soul and our spirit

Great Eternal Love

Great Eternal Love, thank you
For opening my eyes
And giving me life, health and strength
To think good thoughts
And to help the poor and needy
I want to be a help to someone
Let the sunshine my way
When the darkness come, shine on me
Make me a basket of delight to the down cast
And people who have fallen into the pit
The pit of nothingness Alone and afraid
Give me grace to help the human race
Thank you Great Eternal Love

I Know

I know that you love me
Because I can see it
I can feel it
And I know it for sure
Because I am in
Your world of delight and peace...
Your peace that turned me
Into a spiritual light
To my fellow man
All colors and all kinds
They are all mine says the Lord
Be Blessed..

Praises

Eternal love, All everlasting
We lift up your name forever
Father of Light
Creator of Heaven and Earth
Praise your holiness
GOD of Gods healer of the darkness
In the congregation
I will sing songs of praise
I'll play music of delight
Lord heal our unbelief
And help us understand
The right way
Help heal the land and the people
Lord of Love
Give us a well-spring of life
And aid us in trouble
Father save us today tomorrow
And for ever and ever
Thank you Lord of Light
Teach us to live
To love and learn every single day
Those things that are pleasing in your sight
Thank you Father

Healed

I am healed
And I feel brand new
I am here to help you heal
And feel the best you can
You can be healed and delivered
From all pain and sorrow
Look up and smile
Listen to the music
My songs and my prayers
Look up right now
Don't be afraid to feel safe
I'll heal your doubt and unbelief
And your body
Your soul, mind and spirit
Believe me
And Love One Another
And love will come to you
And heal you

A New Praise, Place and Peace

Come with me And touch the sun
Raise your hands high
Smile at GOD
Let GOD be true forever
Be healed by the Supreme Creator of Love
Look into my face you will understand
Selflessness is a place where only
Men of consciousness dwell
A place called Paradise
And a garden of everlasting peace
Can you go with me
Transfiguration is in us all
Treat everyone right and just
And you will go to this place
And Live forever on this new earth
Yes right here if you come right now
Let's live in great peace
And tranquility right now!

The Real Truth

Sin, sickness and death
Are not real for those who believe
The only thing that is truly real is GOD
And all that He stands for
And all those who are like him
So rest assured "Be Holy as I Am Holy"
No fear, no hatred, no sickness and disease
And no death...
The good and the Holy ones
Will just fall asleep
And when they awake
They will live forever
That is the promises of GOD
FOREVER

Love

Love, Love, Love, Love
Love, Love, Love, Love
Love Made me
Love Made me
And Love is in us all...
But some don't' want to show it
And others don't want to know it
Love is in us all...
Love One Another And Live...

Have Faith

Have mercy, have grace
Have peace, have kindness
Have joy, have gentleness
Have temperance, have goodness
Have faith in GOD

Sin No more

Do you want to be healed
Then go
And sin no more...

Ask

Ask and it shall be
Given to you...
Seek and you will find
Knock and the door
Will be open for you...
I know because
It happened for me
I was sad and lonely
And GOD helped me!

GOD Hears

I love the Lord
Because He heard
My crying and dying
Call Him if you are in darkness
GOD is the Light
The Light of Life ...

Change

Come here
Let's talk to GOD for a change...
Do you want to ask him for something?
For money, time or a talent
A place to live or a good place for a job
Do you believe GOD can and will help you?
Have you called unto him
Lets do that right now
Just looked up and say
Father in Heaven listen to my cry
I am so lonely listen to me
Yes God will listen and will hear
He is Father and will be exactly what you need
He'll be a mother, brother, sister to you
And anyone or anything else that you need.
GOD is our friend in need
Try GOD and see. Just say Lord Help Me

Flowers

Love come to me in the morning
I thank you Loving Father,
Thank you for giving me
An understanding heart
To know the way to live
With your lovely daughters
The flowers you planted her on earth
For men, your sons
Help us Lord to heal the flowers you gave us
Only GOD can make a flower
Lord teach us how to
Love your lovely flowers

Songs

Lord listen to my song
I will play the harp, piano, guitar
I will play and sing a song of divine light
And divine Love. Lord let the love
Of my music flow like water brook
Like a stream, a quiet stream
By the lilac bush Oh! Lord
My GOD keep me, keep us
From the evil pit of darkness
Let loving, kindness awaken our souls
And lead is in a path for goodness
Don't let us stumble or fall forever
Let divine music be healing in our minds forever
Father of Heaven please fly to us
Send the evening dove Lord let my music
Chase away the evil spirits, the fallen angels
Lord let the music of peace
And Love everlasting be lifted high
In the heavens. Lord a healing sound
Forever and ever. Praise the Lord with harp,
Piano, guitar and the voices of praise...

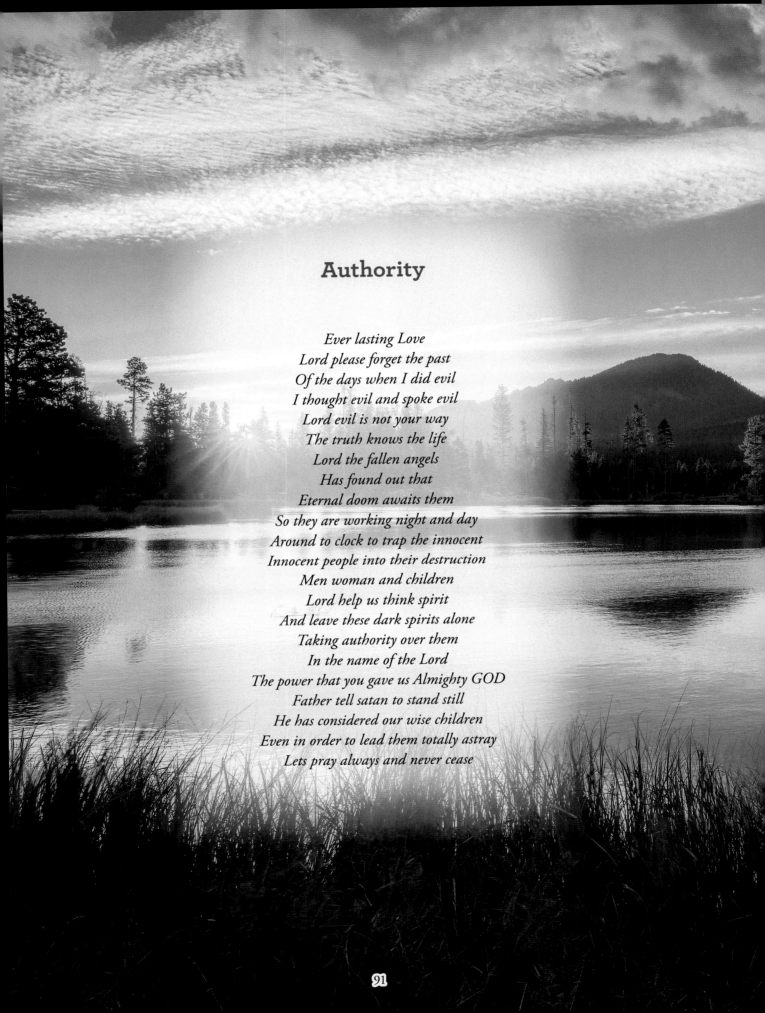

Authority

Ever lasting Love
Lord please forget the past
Of the days when I did evil
I thought evil and spoke evil
Lord evil is not your way
The truth knows the life
Lord the fallen angels
Has found out that
Eternal doom awaits them
So they are working night and day
Around to clock to trap the innocent
Innocent people into their destruction
Men woman and children
Lord help us think spirit
And leave these dark spirits alone
Taking authority over them
In the name of the Lord
The power that you gave us Almighty GOD
Father tell satan to stand still
He has considered our wise children
Even in order to lead them totally astray
Lets pray always and never cease

Man and Woman

Father, I want this woman, Lord I really do
For she seems to be so real to me to be so very sincere
She's the only woman that ever looked at me and smiled
She smiled from her soul. The only woman that said to me
I love you and I felt it through and through. I looked at her so
deeply, so discreetly. I had only one moment to understand
this woman. I would so willingly give her my heart without
doubting. I know this woman deep down inside. She is my
heart and soul. She will always and forever be mine. And I
am hers until. We will live in the love of Jesus Christ. Such love
I can't show her enough love. True love is too deep for man
and woman to understand. The spirit of love can only speak of
love in dimensions. Dimensions of the inner and outer space
and time. This woman is a divine spirit. That meets me in a
divine way with love from the inward and outward expressions
of self. We're in the place where love meets man and woman in
ways unknown. Even unknown to their very mind, spirit, body
and soul Love goes deeper and deeper until they fuse into a
state of our unknown selves Male and female transformed into
the image and likeness of your dear son Father GOD

About the Author

The strangest thing happened to me when I was a little boy about 11 years old. My father was a minister of the Gospel; he was a dignified tall dark and handsome man. His presence was like a King even if he wasn't dressed up. And if he looked at you over those eye glasses in the church; you knew that you were in trouble! I was in big trouble.

Well, one day I was playing up the street from our apartment and there was a condemned building that was being torn down. There was a bulldozer left parked at the demolition site over the weekend. I was all alone playing in the ruins of bricks and rocks. I saw a little old Caucasian man coming towards me. He looked frail and malnourished. He looked at me and said little boy I'm hungry, can you give me something to eat? I said yes, come with me, I walked down the street and he followed me home. I was never taught in those days – "not to talk to strangers". So I took him home with me. We lived on the second floor apartment building. He followed me up the stairs and my mother was cooking fried chicken, mashed potatoes, green beans and cornbread…my favorite dish! I said, "Mama this man is hungry". Then my father walked in I said "daddy this man is hungry". My father politely said – "sir set down at my table". The man set down and began a conversation with my dad – they smiled and talked. My mother and father both enjoyed this man's company, and so did I. When super was over the man left. I was sitting by the window and looked outside to see what direction he was going. But the strangest thing happened; the man never went out of the building. I never saw him leave. I said "Daddy that man never left, he didn't leave this building". My father looked at me and said "son he is gone back to glory, heaven…". I was always visited by Angels. My Angel always comforted me and saved me no matter what happened to me. And I can go on and on about how my Angel healed and helped me all through my life, each and every day of my life. I can go on and on about the Angels of GOD helping me whatever I did in life. I need to really tell you one more truth about a girl friend I had when I was sixteen. I was really in love with this girl. I did wrong with her, I knew it was wrong…she really loved me too. I called her and said meet me in the garden. Fleishman's Garden in Cincinnati, Ohio, that's where I grew up. So she met me there at 7:00 as we agreed. We walked around; laughing and I sang her a song and held her in my arms. It was getting dark by this time. The gardener left in his car and I moved closer to her. My arms were around her as I held her close. In this garden there were 12 foot tall light posts set at different pathways. I said to my girl, look down at the far light-post and tell me what you see? She chilled up and said "let's go". We stood up and I looked again towards the light-post as we started walking out of the garden. I saw a tall being that was taller than the light-post which was at least 12 foot tall. I was not afraid but she was as she ran all the way home. She left her shoes in the street and left me running. The next day I waited for her at the door of the school building where we attended and took classes together. I saw her coming my way up the stairs. She didn't see me but I opened the school door for her to walk in. She looked at me and never said a word. Not hello great to see you or good morning - she never said a word but turned and walked away and I never saw her again, neither did anyone else know what happened to her. To this very day I believe my Angel who I saw that day in the garden saved me from committing a great sin, sex before marriage. So look, all I can say is this – men and brother's do it right. If you really love her-marry the beautiful woman you LOVE.

-------Love Lamone-------

Oh! And brothers, don't forget for GOD is watching you! "Let that flower bloom" A verse in the song by The Emotions – "Flowers"